Bone to

His Bone

J. Shawn Urquhart

Copyright © 2012 Author Name

ISBN-10:1500887013
ISBN-13:9781500887018

DEDICATION

This book is dedicated firstly to my Lord and Savior Jesus Christ. For without him there is no me.

Secondly I'd like to dedicate this book to my mother, Shepherd Mother H. Andrella Urquhart, who has been the source of my strength, inspiration and great encouragement. Thank you for being more than a mother. YOU'VE BEEN A GODLY EXAMPLE. I LOVE YOU!

My children, Corey, Charnelle, J'shawn and Tahjae, I pray that my life and ministry will be the beginning of the greatness you will achieve throughout life.

I'd also like to acknowledge and give thanks to the greatest church on this side of heaven, the "City of Praise Kingdom Cathedral." You've uplifted me in my lowest. I pray the Lord will use me as a vessel to do great things and make you proud. Your weekly demand on my ministry, study and consecration has caused thousands to be blessed.

Table of Contents

Dedication   pg. 3

Chapter 1: The Unusual Assignment   pg. 6
Chapter 2: Watch Your Mouth   pg. 13
Chapter 3: A Second Wind   pg. 17
Chapter 4: Dancing With Broken Bones   pg. 22
Chapter 5: Bad to the Bones   pg. 27

Chapter-1

The Unusual Assignment

Have you ever asked the Lord, why are certain people attracted to me or to my ministry? Have you ever asked the Lord, why do I always give out, more than I get back? Here's my favorite question, WHAT ABOUT ME? Well, in this chapter, the Lord will confirm your assignment as a problem solver. The problem God created you to solve on earth is called your assignment. The mechanic knows that an automobile problem is his connection to you. The lawyer knows that a legal problem is his connection to you. The dentist knows that a tooth problem is his connection to you, and you must know that your assignment is always to someone with a problem. Don't run from it! Embrace it, because you have been anointed for it.

Moses solved problems for the Israelites. Aaron solved problems for Moses. Jonathan was assigned to David. Jonah was assigned to the Ninevites. A handmaiden was assigned to help Naaman get healed. Ruth was assigned to Naomi. Beloved, you are assigned to help someone solve problems. You're the healer for someone sick. You're the life-jacket for someone drowning. You're the ruler over someone unruly. You are the lifter for someone fallen.

That's right, you're called to the people you are called to in order to help them out of trouble. Your assignment isn't to the pretty. Your assignment isn't to the millionaires. Your assignment isn't to the upper echelon of life. Your assignment isn't to the rich and famous. Your assignment is the same as Jesus' assignment. Jesus cries out in St. Luke 4:18-19:

"The Spirit of the Lord *is* upon me, because he hath anointed me to preach the gospel to the poor; he hath sent me to heal the brokenhearted, to preach deliverance to the captives, and recovering of sight to the blind, to set at liberty them that are bruised, to preach the acceptable year of the Lord."

Your anointing is for the homosexual, your anointing is for the liar, your anointing is for the fornicator, your anointing is for the church hopper, and your anointing is for the molester. Someone has to be the gleaner and not just the reaper. The reaper is the one that picks the finest of the crop, the mature of the harvest, the ripest fruit, wherein the gleaner is the one that picks the fruit that which has been overlooked, the crop that was left behind. Jesus said in John 10:16:

"And other sheep I have, which are not of this fold: them also I must bring, and they shall hear my voice; and there shall be one fold, and one shepherd."

Saints you are someone's hope, you're someone's favor, and you're the proof that there is a God. Just as a poem is the proof of a poet, just as the song is the proof of a composer, just as a product is the proof of a manufacturer, you are the proof of Deliverance. You're the proof of healing, the proof of greatness.

You must be comfortable with the anointing upon your life, and most importantly, to whom your anointing is assigned for. Ladies and gentlemen, brothers and sisters great people discern great qualities even in an unfilled state. Successful people are observant people, they are discerners of potential, they spot your strength, your future, distinguish your past from your present, and pick out your failures so that they won't prevent your future. They make clear to you what you cannot clearly understand for yourself. Everyone needs someone that is willing to publicly affirm their relationship in front of people that don't want them to prosper.

God assigns deliverers to us. He places people in our lives to help us. When Satan wants to destroy you, he sends people, but when God wants to bless you he assigns people to you. Moses was assigned to lead the Israelites out of Egypt. Elijah was sent to the widow of Zarapeth to help her faith. If you're sick, look for the man of God that believes in healing. If you are having financial struggles look for the man of God who believes in prosperity. NO ONE FAILS ALONE. If you fail, it will be because you chose to ignore the one assigned to you.

If you're going to be a deliverer you must be a discerner.

Information unfolds the past, situations unfold the present, but revelations unfold the future. You need someone that will help you rid yourself of your yesterday, walk you through your today, and release you into your tomorrow.

Israel's deliverer Moses' name means "drawn out", because he was drawn out of the Nile River by pharaoh's daughter, but also because his main purpose was to lead the children of Israel through the Red Sea. Before try to help someone out of their troubles, you need someone to help you out of yours. You're going to need somebody. You're going to need some help.

Every Adam needs an Eve, every Lot needs an Abraham, every Elijah needs an Elisha, every Elisha needs a Gehazi, every Moses needs a Jethro, every Timothy needs a Paul, every Paul needs a Gamaliel, and every Jesus needs a Simon. The greatest leader needs a leader, same as the greatest father needs a father. Saints of the Most High, "Your next degree of Favor is COMING on Feet."

This was Ezekiel's calling, but his placing was first in a disturbing and conflicting manner. His call was to "Prophesy upon these bones", but he was placed in "the midst of the valley which was full of bones." Verse 1 reveals to us that, it was the "hand of the LORD that place him in this low place.

In my years of teaching on leadership, I have taught that the five -fold ministry represents the hand of God. The index finger represents the prophet, because the job of the prophet is to always point us to God and holiness. The middle finger represents the evangelist, because it's the longest of all fingers, therefore implying outreach. The ring finger represents the pastor, because the pastor is married to the church, and the ring finger is the only finger that has a vein that goes directly to the heart. According to Jeremiah, God gives you pastors according to mine heart, which shall feed you with knowledge and understanding. The pinky finger is the teacher, because the pinky finger is the only finger that fits into the ear without hurting the ear. And then the final finger isn't a finger, it's the Apostle. The Apostle covers all of the aforementioned offices. In other words, we see the hand of God or the hand of the Lord, and it can be a representation of God's movement through your appointed leadership. Remember, that the hand never moves without the mind thinking it first. Your leader, or should I say Godly leaders never move without the spirit and the prompting of the Holy Spirit. Some of you have been placed in uncomfortable places by your senior leadership, know that they have been led by God and that someone needs you where you have been planted.

So when Ezekiel says the hand of the Lord carried him out, we can all agree that there have been times, when God's pastors, teachers, prophets, evangelists or Apostles have placed you in undesirable assignments or questionable atmospheres. Trust the prophetic integrity of your man or woman of God that they would not place you somewhere, where your anointment isn't needed or wouldn't bring results.

His placing had to be conducive to his calling. In general, God places us in atmospheres that will demand results from our anointing. But the problem was that the atmosphere caused Prophet to doubt his anointing. This is why when God asked him "Son of man, can these bones live?" He responded and said, "O Lord GOD, thou knowest." The enemy desires for you to be in your called place, but not have faith in those whom you have been assigned. It's hard to minister to people that you don't trust. It's difficult to prophesy to people whom you don't believe in their possibility to become better. It's hard to anoint individuals whom you are aggravated with. I want to challenge you to empty yourself of every premeditated thought, every word and image that was planted in you by others, so that your assignment will be self-destructed. It's my prayer as I write this devotion that your belief, not in God or yourself is intensed and increased, but your faith in your assignment is evolved.

Think about it this way, if the Prophet had not fulfilled his assignment those bones would still be dry, disconnected and scattered. They would have never reached their potential of being an exceeding great army. Through your leader, God has placed you somewhere that after your anointing has manifested, potential will come forth.

Your assignment whether big or small is equivalent to Peter's in Luke 22:31-32:

"And the Lord said, Simon, Simon, behold, Satan hath desired *to have* you, that he may sift *you* as wheat: But I have prayed for thee, that thy faith fail not: and when thou art converted, strengthen thy brethren. Readers, the anointing to help others, it's birthed from your deliverance."

Take great note that at the beginning of Luke 22, Judas' name is mentioned, saying Satan had entered him. Two men would be sifted, but only one of them would remain. Only one of them would abide. Only one of them would endure. I truly believe that God was using these two examples to deliver to us a principle, and that is: that not everyone who is sifted will be saved. BUT everyone who is saved WILL be sifted! Those who are saved have the precious responsibility to help and save others. I often tell my sons and daughters, that I have failed enough to help you become successful. When God preserves us from certain calamities, not only should we learn from them, but teach from them as well.

Sifting is the process of separating the wheat from the chaff. "Sift" means to harass til nothing but chaff remains. Chaff is the inedible, dry, scaly protective casings of the seeds of cereal grain, or similar fine, dry, scaly plant material such as scaly parts of flowers, or finely chopped straw. ..."Sifted like wheat" is an idiom that in our culture would be equivalent to "taking someone apart". The sifting process was a very violent shaking of the wheat to separate the real fruit from the chaff, after the shaking only the fruit remained. Ladies and gentlemen, brothers and sisters, the shaking in your life, ministry or family will remove the useless and then reveal the greatness. The useless friendships, the useless ideas, the useless people, the useless fellowships, the useless relationships will all be shaken away. The only thing that will remain is greatness.

Simon finds himself in a precarious predicament, because he is never promised to be saved from the sifting, only his faith. Not a single hand is going to be upheld to remove him and place him in some sheltered place. The only thing Jesus was concerned about was preserving his faith, not his flesh. It was his faith, and not his feelings. His faith! Peter is far too valuable to be held immune from the sifting process. If you're going to be anointed, you will be shaken. If you're going to have ministry, you must be shaken. If you're going to have power, you must be shaken. The other day I had a craving for some orange juice and as I began to consume my "no sugar added···100% juice", I noticed a phrase on the side of it that said "SHAKE WELL BEFORE USING." Reader, I need you to hear me clearly your shaking is a sign that God is about to use you.

Remember that Simon/Peter would become the church's first bishop and influence the rest of church history. So Satan's attempt to sift Simon, it was another form of attacking the existence of the church. I want to encourage you by telling you that your level of attack is based on your level of influence. You have influence in this generation. You have influence in your work place. You have influence in the heaven. You have influence with the secular. And the devil is trying to eliminate you, because if you are eliminated then your influence will be useless in the Kingdom of God. Jesus gives Simon an assignment:

"···:.when thou art converted, strengthen thy brethren."

Not "IF" but "WHEN." Peter's recovery was assured before his failure was experienced. Jesus believed in Peter's recovery. Jesus believed in Peter's bounce back. Jesus believed that Peter would improve. Jesus believed that Peter would return. He believed that Peter would be rehabilitated. I'm here to tell you, YOU WILL BOUNCE BACK!!! Your failure is not final. There's still hope!!!

Strengthen means to make stable, place firmly, set fast, fix, make firm, to render constant, confirm one's mind. Jesus was saying to Peter, that after this shaking you will be qualified to minister to others. He was saying someone is going to go through the same thing you have gone through, but you can strengthen them. You may not be able to find the explanation of your suffering in your own life, but the benefits may go to someone else. The wealth earned by your sufferings may be deposited in another's account. You'll be able to stabilize your brother, make your friend firm. If I can help somebody as I pass along, if I can cheer somebody, with a word or song, if I can show somebody, how they're traveling wrong, my living shall not be in vain. If I can do my duty, as a good man ought, if I can bring back beauty, to a world up wrought, if I can spread love's message, as the Master taught, then my living shall not be in vain. My living shall not be in vain, if I can help somebody, as I pass along, then my living shall not be in vain. Stick to your unusual assignment, because your unusual anointing has been tailor made for it.

Chapter-2

Watch Your Mouth

People love to talk. We love to watch talk shows. Everybody seems to have something to say. Everybody has something to talk about. Did you know that the average American has thirty conversations a day and will spend a fifth of their lives talking? This means that in one year if all your conversations were written down with just your words - they would fill sixty six books of eight hundred pages per book. On the average in America - a man will speak twenty thousand words a day. If you are woman - you will speak thirty thousand words a day. Beloved, controlling your words is one of the biggest challenges anyone will face in this life; Solomon writes in Proverbs 18:21:

"Death and life are in the power of the tongue."

Notice that Solomon didn't say that life or death was in the power of the tongue, but rather "death and life *are* in the power of the tongue." Death and Life are both operating every time we speak so we must be more disciplined with our mouths. Every time we speak we are releasing life to one thing and death to another ALL AT THE SAME TIME. If we speak death to poverty we are speaking life to riches. If we speak death to sickness we are speaking life to health. Let's look at it this way, God created the universe just by the power of His words. I wonder what type of world you've created through what you've SPOKEN.

This chapter is to exhort you to monitor what you say and how you say it. Usually it is in the height of our emotions that we say things incidentally, but they are activated because we spoke it. Believe it or not, words can bring life to a dead situation, or words can bring death, destruction, or a whole lot of trouble if misused! James writes more about managing our mouths - than anyone else in the Bible. Let's read James chapter three:

"We all stumble in many things. If anyone does not stumble in word, he is a perfect man, able also to bridle the whole body."
James 3:2 (NKJV)

James says that if you can control your mouth, you'll be perfect. The Greek word for "perfect" does not mean sinless, actually it means to be mature or healthy. So James actually gives the prescription for healthy, mature Christians. Saints of God, when you manage your mouths, it reveals your spiritual maturity and health status. When we manage our words, we also manage our offenses.

Cold words freeze people, warm words loose people, hot words scorch people, cool words calm people, bitter words bite people, kind words sooth people, positive words bring positive results, while negative words bring negative results! Saints of God, there is power, there is great power within our words! Paul writes to the church at Colosse to:

"Let your speech be always with grace, seasoned with salt, that ye may know how ye ought to answer every man."

Colossian 4:6

When I think of seasoning, I think of salt. Salt is flavorful, it preserves. According to Matthew 5, God has called us to be the salt of the earth. In other words, God has called us out of the darkness into the marvelous light to be good "seasoning" in a "tasteless" world. Beloved, God wants us to preserve and add flavor to our family, communities and congregants. The reality is that you can't preserve anybody when you gossip about them! You've got to be careful that you don't say the wrong things in the wrong way, and cause a person to turn totally away from God, and miss out on their purpose - because if they are offended by your communicative actions, then their blood is on your hands!

The devil recognizes the power that's in our mouths, and so many times he convinces us to say the wrong words, just to derail this Gospel train we're riding on. They tell me that it doesn't take much to derail a train. Just a kink, or a break in the tracks, or something that has "intentionally", or maybe "unintentionally" been placed on the tracks, can cause a train to jump its rails and cause a lot of destruction, or maybe even death. Solomon said in Proverbs 18:6,7:

"A fool's lips enter into contention, and his mouth calleth for strokes."

In other words, "A fool's lips bring him strife, and his mouth invites a beating." Another way of saying it is: The words of a talebearer [are] as wounds, and incite a riot.

Here's another chill factor recorded in Matthew 12: 36 (NASV)

"I tell you that every careless word that people speak, they shall give an accounting for it in the Day of Judgment."

Jesus is saying that we will give an account not just for our careless words, but for every word we speak. Words are significant. Words are important. With your words you can build others up and with your words you can cut people down.

There is a command on Ezekiel in Ezekiel 37:7 that will start the revival process:

"So I prophesied as I was commanded: and as I prophesied, there was a noise, and behold a shaking, and the bones came together, bone to his bone"

Please note that while he was prophesying, the bones started coming together. The prophets WORDS created the revival. Note that WHILE the prophet is speaking, order is being established and things are coming together: Your atmosphere is waiting on your command, what you say will determine if your house is will be reunited, your money is be restored, your mind is be renewed, or if your soul will be revived. This happened AS the prophet speaks, not after, not later, not subsequently, not at the end of, but in the current time, the present, the now. God was fulfilling the words of the prophet while he was speaking.

Initially I was confused by the wording of the text, because *verse number 9*, refers to source of this revival as WIND, but then in *verse 10*, he refers to it as BREATHE. Look at it:

⁹Then said he unto me, Prophesy unto the wind, prophesy, son of man, and say to the wind, Thus saith the Lord GOD: Come from the four winds, O breath, and breathe upon these slain, that they may live.
¹⁰So I prophesied as he commanded me, and the breath came into them, and they lived, and stood up upon their feet, an exceeding great army."

The prophet calls for the FOUR winds, North, South, East, and West. If we take the first letters of all this directions we'll spell the word NEWS, or the Good News which is the Word of God. Paul told us in *II Timothy 3:16*:

"All scripture is given by inspiration of God"

The Message Bible says it like this

"Every part of Scripture is God-breathed"

The Contemporary English Version says

"Everything in the Scriptures is God's breathe···"

In doing so, God covers his word in totality. Wind affects the outward, breath affects the inward. So God says before I can revive anything, the WORD MUST BE IN YOU AND my WIND ON YOU.

THINGS ARE COMING TOGETHER, LIFE IS BEING RELEASED!

Chapter-3

A Second Wind

"The hand of the LORD was upon me, and carried me out in the spirit of the LORD, and set me down in the midst of the valley which was full of bones, and caused me to pass by them round about: and, behold, there were very many in the open valley; and, lo, they were very dry. And he said unto me, Son of man, can these bones live? And I answered, O Lord GOD, thou knowest. Again he said unto me, Prophesy upon these bones, and say unto them, O ye dry bones, hear the word of the LORD. Thus saith the Lord GOD unto these bones; Behold, I will cause breath to enter into you, and ye shall live. And I will lay sinews upon you, and will bring up flesh upon you, and cover you with skin, and put breath in you, and ye shall live; and ye shall know that I am the LORD. So I prophesied as I was commanded: and as I prophesied, there was a noise, and

behold a shaking, and the bones came together, bone to his bone. And when I beheld, lo, the sinews and the flesh came up upon them, and the skin covered them above: but there was no breath in them. Then said he unto me, Prophesy unto the wind, prophesy, son of man, and say to the wind, Thus saith the Lord GOD; Come from the four winds, O breath, and breathe upon these slain, that they may live. So I prophesied as he commanded me, and the breath came into them, and they lived, and stood up upon their feet, an exceeding great army. Then he said unto me, Son of man, these bones are the whole house of Israel: behold, they say, our bones are dried, and our hope is lost: we are cut off for our parts." - Ezekiel 37:1-11

What is a second wind? It's renewed energy or strength to continue in undertaking a task; it's the ability needed to maintain a certain momentum in development and progress. A second wind is the return of relatively easy breathing after initial exhaustion during continuous exertion.

I believe that this chapter is dedicated to those who have had the wind knocked out of them; you just went through something that had only one purpose, and that was to slow you down. The enemy of our soul has come to slow us down; he's sending obstacles to lower your momentum, to weaken and to decelerate your stride in ministry and in life. But here and now, I feel a fresh wind, a second wind a new wind is about to blow in your direction. The spirit of slothfulness, lack and depreciation is being lifted and God is about to posture you in your correct strength measurement through this book.

Don't mistake this season of standstill as a season of non-productivity or no progression, for it's really a season of recovery. Recovery is the act of obtaining usable substances from unusable resources; it's when we return to our original condition and atmosphere. Ladies and gentlemen, brothers and sisters, this period of recovery has a specific assignment to help you regain strength;

but also to reveal what God is about to use. Recovery, let's dissect the word. Re means again and again until something is accomplished and or fulfilled, the word cover means to place something on, over or in front as to conceal or protect. Beloved, God is going to keep putting things on you, in front of you or around you, not to kill you, but to protect you. Please know that, "YOUR SEASON OF EXPOSURE AND VULNERABILITY IS OVER."

In medical institutions, recovery is essential to those who have been hurt, cut or damaged. They're usually put in isolation, so that the repair and the healing can be progressive and pure. God's negative response to your prayer wasn't a refusal or a denial, but admittance into recovery. When God said NO, he was disconnecting you from things and/or people that would eventually damage you permanently. Rejection saved your life. People thought they dumped you, but it was for your good. People rejected you, but really they released you.

When we look at Ezekiel 37, there is one word that is repetitious, and that word is bones. Saints of the Most High God, once again bones represent promise. Before Joseph died, he instructed the people to take his bones to the promise land. The promise of the double portion was given to Elisha from Elijah. It must be understood that Elisha had done 7 credible miracles, but when Elisha dies he had only done 13 credible miracles. The 14th miracle wasn't fulfilled until a dead man hit the bones of Elisha. The creation of woman from Adam's bone was the result of God's promise to give Adam a help meet.

Therefore, Ezekiel, the prophet, the seer's vision of scattered, broken, dry bones was a representation of Israel's scattered, broken, and dry promises.

Bones are important to the physiology of man, because the marrow of the bone supplies nutrients for the body. Likewise, promises are important to the body of Christ because they remind us of and represent covenant. This story is the revelation that God was assuring the exiles that the promises of God are secure. When we look at the context of the text, it should be remembered that the exiles had been away from their homeland for so long and they felt disconnected and dry, hence the dry bones. Look at the words in Ezekiel 37 verses 11-14:

'11 Then he said unto me, Son of man, these bones are the whole house of Israel: behold, they say, Our bones are dried, and our hope is lost: we are cut off for our parts.

12 Therefore prophesy and say unto them, Thus saith the Lord GOD; Behold, O my people, I will open your graves, and cause you to come up out of your graves, and bring you into the land of Israel.

13 And ye shall know that I am the LORD, when I have opened your graves, O my people, and brought you up out of your graves,"

God brings the prophet to this valley to give him a vision of Israel's state, V. 1 says that he was:

"Out in the spirit of the LORD, and set me down in the midst of the valley which was full of bones,"

I told you earlier bones represent promises, so when God sets the prophet down in a valley full of dry bones, in actuality it was a valley full of promises. As a matter of fact, I want you to read Ezekiel 37 again and replace the word bone with promise. It will bless your life forever.

The prophet Ezekiel was commanded to:

"Prophesy upon these bones"

So what was the word of the Lord? Verse 5 tells us:

"Behold, I will cause breath to enter into you, and ye shall live"

Now according to this verse the breath/wind wasn't for the flesh, but for the bones. But before the wind was released, the bones had to first come together. There's a spirit of revival and refreshing that's about to come upon the church, but before this can happen, there's going to be a uniting of scattered and dry promises.

Once the wind came, then the following happened to the bones:

Life came. God structures the bones together, so that he could put NEW life back into them. It resembles the same methodology seen in *Genesis 1 and 2*, when God formed man and then created man. He formed man by arranging and assembling man from dust/dirt, and then he created him by breathing into him the breath of life. It should be noted that what was put in man, is what controlled man.

2. *Strength came.* The text says that the bones stood up an exceeding great army. They stood up on their feet, meaning they regained strength and stability. When we experience the purity of promise, then we will never be comfortable lying down. The word stood up in the Hebrew has the same meaning as the word erect or erection, meaning strong enough to perform and produce.

3. *Revelation came.* All in the text we see how these bones were dead dry and scattered, but once the wind hit them, they were an "EXCEEDING GREAT ARMY".

Tonight I know you're in a valley and you see nothing but dryness, you see nothing but lack, you see nothing but devastation, but I'm here to tell you that when GOD gets finished you're going to have life, you're going to have strength and your greatest potential will be seen, for it doth not yet appear···.

This is the bounce back season! This is the hour for you to recover all without fail. You shall recover all. A second wind is about to hit your life: the wind of revival, the wind of blessing, the wind of peace, the wind of joy, is blowing···blow wind blow···.blow wind blow···.

Chapter-4

Dancing with Broken Bones

"Make me to hear joy and gladness; that the bones which thou hast broken may rejoice. *" - Psalms 51:8*

The adult human body has 206 bones. They are important to the natural body because bones provide bodily structure. They allow you to move in many ways. Bones even protect your internal organs, and lot's more.

If you've ever seen a real skeleton or fossil in a museum, you might think that all bones are dead. Although bones in museums are dry, hard, or crumbly, the bones in your body are different. The bones that make up your skeleton are all very much alive, growing and changing all the time like other parts of your body.

Ladies and gentlemen, brothers and sisters, bones are rigid organs that form part of the endoskeleton of vertebrates. They move, support, and protect the various organs of the body. They produce red and white blood cells and store minerals. Bones come in a variety of shapes and have a complex internal and external structure. Almost every bone in your body is made of the same materials: the outer surface of bone is called the **periosteum** (say: pare-ee-os-tee-um). It's a thin, dense membrane that contains nerves and blood vessels that nourish the bone. The next layer is made up of **compact bone**. This part is smooth and very hard. It's the part you see when you look at a skeleton.

Within the compact bone are many layers of **cancellous** bone, which looks a bit like a sponge. Cancellous bone is not quite as hard as compact bone, but it is still very strong. In many bones, the cancellous bone protects the innermost part of the bone, the bone **marrow** (say: mair-oh). Bone marrow is sort of like a thick jelly, and its job is to make blood cells.

But biblically speaking, bones represent something different. Bones represent promise. Joseph instructed the people that when he died to take his bones to the promise land, the double portioned promised to Elisha would have meant that he would have had to do 14 credible miracles, because Elijah did 7. But when Elisha died he had only did 13 miracles until a dead man hit the BONES of Elijah. Ezekiel's command in Ezekiel 37 was to speak to the dry bones; the creation of WOMAN (Adam's Help) was a result of God removing a bone from ADAM. Bones represent promise. In Psalms

51 when David talks about:

"... The bones which thou hast broken...."

He is not speaking of a literal crushing of his broken bones, but he's speaking of some broken promises. Sometimes repentance and deliverance will never come until we embrace the revelation of what that sin has cost us.

This is why David declares in verses 2 and 7 reads:

"Wash me throughly from mine iniquity, and cleanse me from my sin."
"Purge me with hyssop, and I shall be clean: wash me, and I shall be whiter than snow."

There are two Hebrew words that are used to denote washing and cleansing. One word means to clean superficially, to wash the surface, such as cleaning off a table or washing the hands. But there is another word that is used to refer to washing thoroughly, to cleaning beneath the surface, to cleansing through and through. Saints of the Most High God, David's concern is not only for ceremonial cleansing, that would qualify him for worship with God's people. He was more concerned with the inner cleansing that would renew the promises of God. That's why he states in verse 8 again:

"Make me to hear joy and gladness...."

The Psalmist prays that God would restore the promise, but not just the manifestation of the promise, but the hearing of the promise. Paul wrote in Romans 10:17:

"So then faith [cometh] by hearing, and hearing by the word of God."

I like the JB Philips Translation of this scripture:

"Belief you see can only come from hearing the message,

and the message is the word of Christ. "

So when David requested to:

"Make me to hear joy and gladness . . . . "

He was really saying IF I CAN HEAR THE PROMISE I CAN BELIEVE IN GOD AGAIN. He requests the hearing of the WORD, the hearing of the PROMISE, send a prophet, send an email, send a text message, and send a messenger, BUT SEND YOUR WORD.

So, when he speaks of his bones as having been broken, he alludes to the extreme grief and overwhelming distress to which he had been reduced, because there is no promise being fulfilled and because he cannot hear the voice of God. He wanted to hear the voice of love, the voice of promise, the voice of forgiveness, the voice of pardon, not the voice of anger and condemnation. God now condemned him. The law condemned him. His own conscience condemned him. But Paul said in Romans 8:1:

"There is therefore now no condemnation to them which are in Christ Jesus, who walk not after the flesh, but after the Spirit."

One theologian says "That the bones which thou hast broken may rejoice is that which have been crushed or broken by the weight of sin. The word "rejoice" means here, be free from suffering. The prayer is that the burden which had crushed him might be removed. The burden was great and overpowering - such was crushing him; breaking all his "bones.", breaking all his promises.

Let's look at the words of David:

"The bones which THOU hast broken."

He that made our bones and placed them in their several places, and tied them together with ligaments, and covered them with flesh; he that keepeth all our bones from breaking; is the same one that has been moved to break them. Broken bones by a cunning hand

may be set again and returned to their former use and strength.

In psychology, there is a pain of setting these bones again: although dislocated bones may be put in joints, and though bones broken may be set again, it is not done without pain and great extremity to the patient.

After every breaking there is a settling, after every breaking there is a rejoicing, after every breaking there is a restoration. After you have suffered a while, make you perfect, establish, strengthen, settle you, we are troubled on every side, yet not distressed; [we are] perplexed, but not in despair; Persecuted, but not forsaken; cast down, but not destroyed; it didn't kill you. The sin didn't kill you. You repented just in the Knick of time. You got yourself together right in the Knick of time.

Beloved, God is healing your promise. He's making you ready for your promise. He's qualifying you for the promise. Your prayer should be, Lord prepare me to be a sanctuary, pure and holy tried and true, and with thanksgiving I'll be a living sanctuary, just for you. You're about to hear again, you're about to see again, you're about to dance again, you're about to rejoice again. The weights didn't break the promise, the confusion didn't break the promise, the rumor didn't break the promise, and the hell didn't break the promise. The promise is still alive. The promise is still good. The promise is still going to happen. God still will heal. God will still deliver. Jeremiah writes in Jeremiah 29:11, "For I know the thoughts that I think toward you," saith the LORD, "thoughts of peace, and not of evil, to give you an expected end." God still has a plan for you. God still has a purpose, and we know that all things work together for good.

When I studied the treatment for a broken bone, it reminded me of our Lord and Savior Jesus Christ. To treat the broken bone, the doctor needs to know what kind of fracture it is. That's where X-rays come in handy. X-rays give doctors a map of fractures so that they can set the bones back in their normal position.

With breaks in larger bones or when a bone breaks in more than two pieces, the doctor may need to put in a metal pin — or pins — to help set it. Scriptures make it clear that they put nails in his hand and nails in his feet.

Then they would put a cast on that leg or the special bandage that will keep the bone in place for the 1 to 2 months, it will take for the break to mend. Before they put Jesus' body in the grave, they wrapped him up in grave clothes. Before he got up out of the grave, he folded the napkin and neatly put the grave clothes in their place.

Chapter 5

Bad to the Bone

²¹And the LORD God caused a deep sleep to fall upon Adam, and he slept: and he took one of his ribs, and closed up the flesh instead thereof; ²²And the rib, which the LORD God had taken from man, made he a woman, and brought her unto the man. ²³And Adam said, this is now bone of my bones, and flesh of my flesh: she shall be called Woman, because she was taken out of Man." - Genesis 2:21-23

My assignment in this chapter is to minister to your esteem, to minister prophetically to your self-value, to declare to your inner most being that your stock has increased and that you must start viewing yourself as God sees you, and not how you and others see you. Ladies and gentlemen, brothers and sisters, the real you is about to manifest. The uniqueness of your anointing is about to break forth. The rareness of your revelation is about to be heard. You are a heaven original, a divine design and you will lower your value by compromising your uniqueness.

I came to preach to some people who have suppressed who you really are, to make others comfortable. During this time of manifestation, you will either draw some by your uniqueness or drive others out by the challenge. As a matter of fact separation and aloneness seek greater self-value than a colossal of people. (Give the story of diamond and CZ)Peter says it like this in 1 Peter 2:5:

⁵Ye also, as lively stones, are built up a spiritual house, an holy priesthood, to offer up spiritual sacrifices, acceptable to

God by Jesus Christ."

Take recognition to the words of Peter, he's indicated that a spiritual house is built with stones and not bricks. Bricks are uniformed, but stones are unique because they don't come in the same size, shape or color. Paul told the church at Corinth to:

" ······:be perfectly joined together in the same mind and in the same judgment."

I want to challenge you to stop allowing people to posture you in a place that's not equivalent to your self-perception. Ladies and gentlemen, brothers and sisters people will only treat you according to the demonstration of your self-worth. If you are attracting people who don't appreciate you, maybe it's because you don't demonstrate that you appreciate yourself. If you're attracting people who don't celebrate you, maybe it's because you don't celebrate yourself. If you're attracting people that don't praise you, perhaps it's because you don't praise yourself. Usually the ill treatments of others are a result of 1 of 2 things:

1. They underestimate your true worth.

2. Or they are intimated by your true worth.

Genesis chapter 2 proves the woman/Eve was created by God, but from bones, a man's bone. Bones are important to the body. Bones give the body structure and definition. Without bones, the muscles would be useless. Bones provide a levy system so that the muscles can produce work through progressive motion. A bone can never operate properly, if it's forced in and not fitted in. They are constructed and formed to fit into certain joints to secure the functioning and the mobility of the human body. When the bone is forced to do what it's not fitted to do, it causes pain and great discomfort. We must endeavor to stop trying to fit and function in a place that was not created for us. When opportunities open, they bring with them the right timing and the right atmosphere for you to be productive.

As in previous chapters in this book, when we look at biblical references of bones, we see continuity that they represent promise.

In Ezekiel 37, the wind of God didn't blow until the bones came together. When God created man, he was made from the dust of the earth. Dust is a by-product of dried dirt. Dust is less than dirt and it can be easily displaced by a gust of wind. Yet God, in his infinite wisdom collected dust and made man. He then breathed in to man's nostrils and gave this dust (man), this collection of dirt, the breath of life. God tells this new creature, which now has skin, hair, muscle and bone to have dominion over the earth and to subdue it. (Inspite of your dirt, God gave you dominion, a kingdom position)

Although this creation was impressive, it was also incomplete. When the Lord surveyed the situation, his decision was to produce a "help" for Adam. This word Help means "one who assists another to reach fulfillment". It speaks of the idea of a completer. The word "meet", refers to one who "is suitable" or corresponds to. In other words, when God envisioned a "HELPMEET" for Adam, he was creating someone that could fill up the lacking in his life.

Now, God converts the garden into a massive operating room as he conducts an orthopedic surgery on ADAM/MAN. God took the rib bone from Adam and made Woman. God made both man and woman, but woman was not made from dust. She was made from the rib bone. This bone that she was made from has the highest and more advanced substance of calcium than any other bone in man's body. Calcium is the strongest and hardest substance in the human body. Look at how God does this phenomenon. He puts man to sleep, and reaches into man, and pulls out the strongest part of his anatomy, a bone!!

There is no scriptural reference that Adam had any knowledge of this divine procedure, but when he woke up and saw WO-MAN, he immediately identified her as:

"This is now bone of my bones"

God is about to make you the prayers of someone else.

Theologians have said that this bone that was taken away from Adams body is the sternum or the chest bone. The uniqueness about this particular bone is that it protects the heart, chest, lungs and major blood vessels, it's a small, long, flat, bony plate shaped like a capital "T", located in the center of the chest. It connects the rib bones via cartilage bringing both sides of the rib cages together. All the vital organs including lungs are surrounded by this bone. The body is built so that before a vital organ could suffer damage, the bone will allow itself to be broken or even crushed.

You were made from the highest quality. How can you have low self-esteem, and you've been through what you've been through and survived? You've been made from good stock. You were made in His image. When God made you, He made the cream of the crop. You've been wonderfully and fearfully made. You are somebody. We are his people, and the sheep of his pasture. Doesn't matter who dumped you. Doesn't matter who laughed at you. You're coming up and going higher.

So if no one else celebrates you, celebrate yourself. If no one else pats you on the back, pat yourself on the back. If no one else takes you out, take your own self out. If no one else gives you thumbs up, give yourself the thumbs up. Never doubt yourself, and know that you are bad to the bone. Allow me to use the words of George Thorogood's song, "BAD TO THE BONE" and revise it for our illustration purpose:

On the day you were born, the angels all gathered 'round. But hell gazed in wide wonder, at the joy the angels had found. After several attempt to kill you, Satan spoke up and said, we better leave this one alone. For he could tell, you were bad to the bone.

NO WEAPON FORMED AGAINST YOU SHALL PROSPER!

Apostle Urquhart ministers under a heavy Apostolic, prophetic and deliverance anointing. It's has allowed him to draw audiences from many denominations wherever he's traveled. He's a highly sought after revivalist, consecrator and conference speaker. Countless of thousands have been blessed, through this ministry of revelation and inspiration.

Besides being the only son of Elder H. Andrella Urquhart, he is also the father of two beautiful daughters and two handsome sons.

It is our greatest hope that you've enjoyed reading this book, and that it's inspired you to do great things in life while pushing those in need of blessings you come across, to do the same.